Wax
Ian Burnette

smith|doorstop

Published 2018 by Smith|Doorstop Books
The Poetry Business
Campo House,
54 Campo Lane,
Sheffield S1 2EG
www.poetrybusiness.co.uk

Copyright © Ian Burnette 2018
All Rights Reserved

ISBN 978-1-912916-07-4
Typeset by Utter
Printed by Biddles

Smith|Doorstop books are a member of Inpress: www.inpressbooks.co.uk. Distributed by NBN International, Airport Business Centre, 10 Thornbury Road Plymouth PL 6 7PP.

The Poetry Business gratefully acknowledges the support of Arts Council England.

Contents

5	Introduction X
6	Explanation No. 6
7	Wax
8	Red
9	Harvests
11	The Lede
12	High Noon
13	A Boy is a Gun
14	On Leaving
15	Rot Land
16	Sty
17	Moonlight
18	Advice
19	Sunshine
20	Kept
21	Crumpled-Up Note for Franz Wright
22	No Ohio
24	Acknowledgements

Introduction X
after Terrance Hayes

I am in love with reversal. How a room is just a moor
        looking the other way, or a moor in a doom mood
                as it locks a liquored wanderer beneath the heather.

Gink nus, sun king, pin snip, pools sloop. I can't make
        heads or tails of noon, her face of perfect symmetry.
                Somewhere, not here, if you pull a dead girl from the river

and hang her on a drying line, you can bring her
        back to life. Somewhere, the mystery is not what will
                come in the night but how to put the body back together.

Dog god, drib bird, ate eta. It's almost like words,
        the body, same symmetry and violence. What I touch
                turns to gold. What I touch turns to dust. The blue wire

is connected to the blue wire. The red wire wants to drown all in its sight.

Explanation No. 6

After swimming pools, my second true fear:
other people are my hallucinations.

It's no wonder. My parents ruined me.
When I was a child, whatever I named
was.

I wanted a deck of cards.
I wanted a violet ray.
I wanted someone to hold me down in the grass.

No, I didn't ask for you, but it can't be ruled out.

Parts of us have a secret will.
Proof?
A brine kicks in your chest.
Without your permission, you are alive.

Parts of us have no mercy for the others.
Proof?
Despite myself, I turn to face the water,
jump.

I break the plane of darkness (washed in sun).

Wax

I have no patience for the void, all talk and tinsel promises
of clean slates and genius copy from the muse
delivered by zigzag of lightning. I learned early: if by magic, then fake.
Nothing exists untethered. Not even islands,
which rise on the whim of vents below.
Radio waves from the '60s now return to Earth.
The lab monster won't wake until you say its father's name aloud.
Once I wanted to be a famous magician.
In Ms Q's homeroom the other kids watched
as I charmed a dollar bill to float above my desk. How easily I had them,
egg-blank faces on all but Ms Q, who glowed
or else pretended to. Grown, I am aware this is mostly what people do and so
look always for the string
held by a drop of wax beneath the thumb, hung over-ear,
then tacked to the face of the crumpled bill
which, as I cast my hand downward, would rise.

Red

Beware its advocates everywhere:
Surgeons. Confectioners. The criminal-insane,
bald or behind an impervious mask,
who long to press the big, blush button
and watch the world tatter from afar.
Doctor Doom, Death Star, Nazi Hugo Drax:
so far no blast (one is inclined to say,
regarding the expanse of virgin blacktop).
Or maybe the bomb fell already,
no mind behind its invisible, dread-less descent.
No threat. No time, then, to prepare the blood,
or for the obligatory act of defense.
No teacher crooning *Kids, get under the desk.*

Harvests

We used to play pirates.

In an empty field
near my father's house

I turned the dirt
by hand, stole mud-quartz

and tar beetles,
once, a penny spoon

pulled from the dirt
like a copper thorn from a wrist,

unsealing a ring of red.
I had my small treasure

and the seed man his
answer: a lease of the land.

My father signed
and shook his shirt-cuffed hand

on the promise
of yellow gold, a flower

that by September
would drip and shine, give oil.

Bud crossed our field
like a floodlight. Stalks rose

and masked secret glades,
left narrow entries

to the slant passageways
where they walked, carrying

the girl into our field,
before they made her open up.

The Lede

Everywhere were ads for Girl with a Pearl Earring, on-tour –
the portrait's likeness bulb-lit on black cab roof billboards
and hung in phone boxes. *Who's that?*
the masses asked. The Dutch master's daughter? His whore?

Those evenings I walked crosstown by way of churchyards
where gravestones of the famous stood defaced
by marker epitaphs: names and slurs and ink-dark stars.
Each entry marked a fiction. Nonsense, corpse after corpse

we fake the lede and damn the source, and adore the dead
far better than we know them. A boy I vaguely knew jumped
off a roof, died. It was strange, I felt as each day passed
somehow closer to him. Now I remember the good times

he and I had on Ms Q's Civil War history tour, 6th grade –
on the bus to Camden Downs, or was it Daufuskie Island?

High Noon

It's true, sometimes
        only the horses survived.

Not even a hold-up man would put holes in a
stallion that might later carry him.

A town drains through the floorboards.

        The mare, caparisoned with blood,
bows. She drinks from the bath.

A Boy is a Gun

Strange, how over and over again the west is won.
I used to wake up a boy, but now I wake up a gun.
A masked man holds me like the woman he loves.

We ride in a Cadillac the color of licorice. It hums
and shines in the sun, its whisper like a religion.
Strange, how over and over again the west is won

by the glow of the twenty dollar, the motion of
fresh-pressed cargo in the night. Well on his way,
a masked man holds me like the woman he loves

behind a house bathed in search-light. He works
a bullet inside me with the edge of his thumb.
Strange, how over and over again the west is won

and not won. I am first the match, second its fire,
and then the match that sets the house ablaze.
A masked man holds me; like the woman he loves

I am already asleep and deep in a dream as explicit
as something red and damned, lying on the ground.
Strange, how over and over again the west is won.
A masked man holds me like the woman he loves.

On Leaving

Not loving
        or loveless.
Like boarding-up the windows of a house
        before a storm.
Like a mother
        in a war movie
waving goodbye to her children
        as they slide away into the distance
on an air raid train.
Like an air raid. But when the planes
        open up to the sky,
to their surprise,
        nothing falls from inside them.

Rot Land

Each day stands in one of three hemispheres, all equally grim

except the fourth
which is perfectly bright and can be seen if you are chosen.

If you're wondering – no.
Fear is the ball God threw me to play with when he left for the store.

Yes, in time some of it becomes fun.
Likelihoods diminish. The stomach shrinks to match.

There is a pride that comes of needing less and less.
I am so slight I dazzle myself.

My mother once bought my love with chocolate and fizzy drinks.
I've since sworn them off. I've changed.

On Monday this rot tooth will be fit with silver.

Sty

Say, a farm's stage of sludge and slop neatly fenced
        or the eyelid's clot of cells, the hot pin that swelled
as, in tears, I cleared a path to the door.

My mother had screamed, called me half pig
        half child, my room the sty, and was semi-right.
Though she kept house with the zeal of a naval officer:

hands and knees, hospital corners. Fabuloso
        All-Purpose: our purple de facto Jesus. Sundays
I was to stay inside until the tile shone cyanide-white.

I learned nothing from discipline. Okay, I learned
        I prefer chaos. I learned to trust in the dark-horses
of disarray: say, when pigs fight in the sty

and leave the likeness of a prophet drawn in mud,
        or when M heaved the bowling ball
into the air. Haphazard, it arced

then struck the edge of the lane.
        She shut her eyes, but I saw the ball: spectral
as it hooked left and swept ten pins away.

Moonlight

A question about predators in dreams. The wolf circles. By the killer's knock, I can tell that he is me. So how do they leap, if not with my permission?

Advice

You should not try heroin. My aunt shot up once
and died.
The first time I took pills for fun I thought of her.
Not of her then, her, but her
the night she visited my mom as a yellow balloon.
I stood in front of the mirror
and let lime slush fall from my mouth into the sink.

I'm sitting beside my aunt Marsha's suitcase
right now.
I won't say what she wrote in all these letters.
She was a private person – loved God, her family,
and peach pie,
the kind of girl who wanted to die.

Drugs are for those
who want to throw the world away,
I was told as a kid
by those who cast their own displeasure on the dead
and saw it reflected
in the chrome of this or that casket.

I do the same – the opposite.
What if, by injection, she meant to enter her life?
What if the body is a signpost
marking a farm road, illuminated when a car passes
and so a sliver of field revealed, but if not, then not –

whereas the body that swallows a coal
shines, and can aim the light at what it pleases.

Sunshine

Is a wonderful drug. Activates the emergency exit in my head.
A man wearing a balaclava screams at me through the window of his Mercedes.

Kept

As she kept me that winter – the acres
mine to wander. The grand house.
The green room of her gem-box.
I pressed cider and smoked in the garden.
She worked until evening.
Then I was hers.
She rose like black water. Fucked me.
Hung a bell around my neck.
Once used to hail servants
from distant rooms, it rang then for me.
No, for my mistress
and so for me. My only task was to call her.

Crumpled-Up Note for Franz Wright

It's spring in Ohio and I just turned nineteen.
I can't even believe what I feel like today –
climbing the hill with a paper bird bone between my fingers,
grandfather's gold ring crowned in smoke.
Something is growing behind me. A pair of misspelled wings.
The house on the corner is grey like a pill.
Looks like a man with a gun in his mouth.

No Ohio

No TV light cast by house windows. No honey-disk sun or shadows of
                              silos lowering with it.
No fluorescent roadside ice cream parlor painted medicine blue.
No cornfields lit by tractor light, combines roving in the dog-gum night.
No you and me sitting here beneath the dark slice of the moon.
Many things are invisible until you name them – the Lightless-Defunct.
I have the nervous system of a hummingbird, you said, and the blank of your
                              neck flushed into sight.

Acknowledgements

Thanks to the print and online publications in which versions of these poems first appeared: *Best New Poets*, *The Forward Book of Poetry*, the *Adroit Journal*, *Introduction X* (Smith|Doorstop 2017) and poets.org. Thanks also to the institutions that have given me a place and time to write, and where I met my favourite teachers and dearest friends: Kenyon College, Kenyon Review, South Carolina Governor's School for the Arts and Humanities, Goldsmiths – University of London, Poetry Society and The Arvon Foundation.

Thanks to Mamie Morgan and Scott Gould. They taught me how to write. Thanks to Andy Grace, who made time for me and my poems, even when he had none. Thanks to Richie Hofmann, Janet McAdams, Mike McGriff, Emily Nason, Natalie Shapero and Phoebe Stuckes for their help with this manuscript; to Emily Birnbaum, Maggie Doyle, Anna Libertin and Frances Saux for their ceaseless love and support; to my mom and dad. And to Meg, who gets me.